Paralegal 411:

Tips Tricks and Timesavers for the Litigation Paralegal

By Dee Thompson

Table of Contents

Introduction

After almost 40 years in the paralegal profession, I have figured out a few things. I would never call myself an "expert" but I have some wisdom to pass along that I think will be helpful to newbies.

This is not meant to be a comprehensive textbook. This book will be most useful to:

- a litigation paralegal getting ready to start a first job
- a litigation paralegal who has been on the job less than a year
- a litigation legal assistant or paralegal trying to help their attorney be more organized

I finished my paralegal education at the National Center for Paralegal Training in May of 1985, before many of you were born. At that time, I think it was the only paralegal training school in the South, that anyone knew about. That was long before the days of looking up stuff on Google. Every student there had a bachelor's degree in something else but had decided to go to paralegal school in hopes of getting a job. I had an undergraduate degree in Drama, but I couldn't find work as a playwright. (Don't laugh, my degree came in handy at times when I was a paralegal.)

I trained to be a corporate paralegal. Then I left Atlanta and went home to Knoxville where I quickly learned there were very few of those jobs. My first job was as a litigation paralegal at a very old, well-established insurance defense law firm. Nothing in my paralegal program had really prepared me for that job. I barely knew the difference between a plaintiff and a defendant.

The firm had very little idea what to do with a paralegal, so I did everything. I made copies. I made coffee. I ran to the courthouse and filed pleadings and got copies of pleadings. I also got sandwiches for everyone in all day depositions in our conference room. I did whatever they asked me to do, just glad to be working. Finding the first job can be a big hurdle. (See page 17 for some tips on where to find that first job.)

One of the senior partners at the firm told me soon after I started "A young pup just out of law school is useless for the first year. He should be paying US that first year!" He glared at me as he was speaking, and I got the message loud and clear: ditto for paralegals. *You should be paying us.* (Never mind that I was making so little I had to get financial help from my parents.) He also said "Women can't do legal research!" and "No laughing here! This is a law firm!" so I quickly realized that he was a curmudgeon and I tried not to let anything he said upset me.

My training as a corporate paralegal was completely wrong to prepare me for life as a litigation paralegal, so I had to adapt and improvise every.single.day for years. There was only one other paralegal at my first job and she was paranoid that if she helped me, they would fire her and replace her with me… so she refused to help me. I got help from everyone else – the secretaries, the young associates, even sometimes the law clerks, who knew useful stuff like where to find the fastest cheap lunches in the downtown area. The legal secretaries who had been there for years were really helpful at keeping me calm, because I was always aware that the consequences of me making a mistake could cost the client a lot of money and cost me my job. I remember one kindly older secretary saying "Dee his bark is worse than his bite. Don't let him upset you!" I remember very few days that were easy.

To give you an idea of what a different time it was, I didn't have a computer at that first job, or even a typewriter. I had to get permission from the office manager to send a fax – and that was "high tech" for the time. I had to wear formal clothes, and pantyhose. The phrase "business casual" had not been coined yet.

I had been working as a paralegal for 8 years before I got a job where I had my own computer on my desk.

At my second job I was working on a lot of different kinds of cases – products liability, collections, even divorces, so there was a learning curve there, too. I kept tennis shoes under my desk for when I had to run to the courthouse, and I had to go often. Everything was filed on paper.

Eventually, after working for large and small firms for years, I realized that if there had been a book like this when I started out, it would have been helpful. I want this book to be helpful to you, whatever your level of experience. I used to go to CLE seminars and hope that out of hours of PowerPoints and speeches I might come away with one or two useful tips that would help me in my day-to-day work life. Sometimes I didn't walk out with any useful knowledge.

There are books out there that advise you on how to do a lot of this stuff but here's what makes this little book different. Many times, those textbooks are written by attorneys, or by paralegals who have only had one job at one firm. I've worked for big firms with hundreds of attorneys, and I've worked for sole practitioners. There is a vast difference between someone who is teaching something academically and one who is advising you in a practical, *this is how I've done it a million times*, boots on the ground kind of way. If you are reading this, I assume you already know what a paralegal is, and someone has schooled you about esoterica like career goals, ethics, research, etc.

This little book is meant to be completely free of filler and fluff. It's a practical guide, and it's not intended to be comprehensive.

That said, one of the key attributes of paralegal success is being flexible. The paralegal role, ideally, should be different from the administrative assistant role, but not all attorneys care about that. I still see job ads where paralegals are asked to transcribe dictation and get the [paper] mail out. You will have to decide if you will refuse to do administrative work or be a team player. If administrative work offends you, you may need to look for a different job. On the other hand, if it's a sole practitioner who can't afford a secretary and a paralegal, and you pitch in and help do everything, in a few years you might find yourself in the office manager role. At both my corporate paralegal jobs I was told on day one I would have to do all my own administrative work. The tradeoff was that I would never have to bill time. I felt like it was a fair tradeoff.

No matter what kind of job you're in – whether a small firm, large firm, plaintiff's practice or defense practice, you need to have these attributes, or develop them quickly:

- Super well-organized
- Meticulous about the details
- Able to analyze information quickly
- Able to learn on your own
- Customer service oriented; in other words, able to talk professionally to clients
- Willing to go the extra mile, to work overtime if necessary
- Always aware of time and the need to bill every task, every day [in a defense firm you bill everything but usually not in a plaintiff's firm -

HOWEVER, in a plaintiff's firm you still have to be productive even if you don't bill]

The role of the litigation paralegal is still evolving. As files are stored in the cloud and offices go paperless and more and more folks work from home, the profession is changing, and adapting to change is a key to surviving. It's not just about technical skills, though. As long as there are law offices, a paralegal will need to be organized, efficient, and more. Keep reading if you are curious as to whether or not you have the right attributes for the paralegal life.

Dee Thompson

Attributes of a Paralegal

I am on several Facebook groups for paralegals and every day there is someone who posts and says *I am thinking about going to paralegal school, any advice?*

Oftentimes the inquiries come from people who are already educated and erudite, but who aren't happy in their careers, or they think after a few years as a paralegal they will be making a seven-figure salary and given a corner office at a law firm. I see the same advice given over and over: be organized, persistent, detail-oriented, etc.

READ THIS CAREFULLY: Do NOT expect a seven figure salary until you've put in at least 5 years and even then, know that very few firms pay that well.

I decided to write an article for people who think they might want to be paralegal but they aren't sure, and they don't really know anything about the profession. I've included it below.

You think The Law sounds glamorous and exciting. It sounds like a noble and honorable profession. You've watched TV shows like Boston Legal or So Help Me Todd or maybe you've seen the movie Erin Brockovich and you feel you've got a pretty good handle on it. In shows and movies, you see paralegals running around looking like junior executives, seemingly the power behind the throne, so to speak. You think you have a pretty good idea of what a paralegal does.

Wrong. If you've never worked in a law office you have no idea what a paralegal does.

I have been a Litigation paralegal since 1985. I've worked for small firms and big firms and sole practitioners. I've worked in two corporate law departments. I've also done marketing for law firms. I've been treated like an associate and like a secretary. For years, I kept a pair of tennis shoes in my desk drawer so I could run to the courthouse and file pleadings – now, thankfully, most things can be filed online. I've been tasked with making thousands of copies of records, picking up lunch for everyone in a deposition, and writing voir dire questions for jury selection.

Before you read any further, ask yourself the questions below. If the answer to any of these questions is no, stop reading. Forget paralegal school. Do something else.

Can you sit at a computer for 8 hours a day?

Are you highly organized and meticulous about details?

Can you type at least 55 wpm?

Can you be happy in a job where no matter how hard you work you will likely not advance, even though you may make more money after 5-10 years? [Only maybe 10% of all paralegals make a six-figure salary]

Are you fine with being treated like a secretary? [some attorneys will always view you as a glorified secretary and have you typing up dictation and/or standing at a copy machine for hours]

Would you be able to be businesslike and polite while on the phone with a screaming client?

Can you forgive a supervisor who couldn't care less about your birthday or your relationship issues or any personal issue you might have? [some attorneys are like that, not all]

Are you okay with being asked to pick up lunch for everyone in the office, or pick up an attorney at a car dealership, or make coffee for your attorney every morning? [in smaller towns, at smaller firms, they may ask you to do a lot of things you think shouldn't be in your job description]

Do you have excellent writing and research skills?

Are you fine with the idea of writing down every single task you do, every single day?

Are you good with working all weekend or on Thanksgiving or Christmas if your boss is getting ready for trial, and I mean 8-12 hours a day, at the office?

Do you know Excel, Powerpoint, Adobe and Word, intermediate or advanced level?

Do you speak Spanish or would you be willing to learn?

If you answered [honestly] yes to all those questions, keep reading.

Types of Litigation Paralegals

Did you know there are many kinds of Litigation Paralegals? It's not all about lawsuits and courtroom drama. Only Litigation Paralegals get to [sometimes, maybe once a year] go to trial. I have been a Litigation Paralegal since 1985.

You will have to decide what kind of law appeals to you. Below are the kinds of paralegals out there, and most of these descriptions are taken from actual job ads:

Litigation:

- Obtains, reviews, analyzes, and summarizes legal documentation pertaining to cases.
- Schedules depositions and other meetings with clients, witnesses, experts, opposing counsel, court reporters and others.
- Identifies, locates, interviews, and evaluates potential experts and sends expert packages to parties for review.
- Tracks requests for documents and regularly follows up on progress of receipt.
- Regularly reviews files and proactively works to move cases forward.
- Documents files and updates clients when necessary regarding status of case.
- Participates in all aspects of discovery and file or trial preparation as required by supervisor.
- May prepare draft discovery documents.
- Maintains an expert database and researches opposing counsel's experts.
- Makes travel arrangements and provides directions and other necessary information to attorney.

- Performs research pertaining to legal issues and precedents related to particular cases.
- Files documents with the various courts.
- Performs clerical duties such as typing and filing to the extent required to produce work product or assure proper organization of case files.
- Enters billable time into computer on a daily basis. [you have to write down every task, daily, if you are in a defense firm]
- Ensures all functions are performed in exact accordance with applicable client guidelines.

In the **Litigation** category there are many different subspecialities. Here are some:

Personal injury – people (plaintiffs) are injured in a car accident – these are the kinds of attorneys who often run commercials on the local TV stations. Paralegals there are often handling over 100 cases at a time. They are often called Case Managers and it can be very stressful to work at a place where they want cases moved through the pipeline and settled very quickly.

Medical Malpractice – when someone sues a doctor or medical facility – often these are very complex cases. Most paralegals don't get these kinds of cases as newbies, unless they already have some experience in the medical field first.

Business – lawsuits involving business disputes. Often these cases involve a company breaking up and executives arguing over who gets what and/or who is responsible for problems. They can be quite complex and document intensive.

Employment – when someone sues their employer for discrimination or harassment of some kind. For example, a worker is pregnant and gets terminated because they miss some training.

Employers aren't allowed to discriminate against pregnant employees, or disabled employees. I have more than 15 years of experience in this area. It's a fascinating subsection of the law.

Workman's Compensation -- a person injured at work sues to get money. Often, workers are not given enough time off of work to heal or not reimbursed for the medical bills. Sometimes the dispute is whether or not the injury is truly an on-the-job injury.

Family Law – Paralegals handle all the paperwork involved in divorces, child custody disputes, adoptions. There is usually a lot of client contact and clients often are unhappy. You have to not let very emotional clients get to you. You have to be very kind but detached.

Contracts – if you can analyze a contract and competently break it down and understand its nuances, you will likely never have to look for a job for very long. Contracts rule the business world and understanding them is truly valuable in the job market.

Construction - when a building goes up there is usually a contractor and a number of subcontractors, and disputes are common. Cost overruns and sloppy work from subcontractors can affect the reputation of the contractor. This is a challenging area because it often involves contracts, liens, bonds, and more.

Intellectual Property – who owns the rights to a song lyric? Who rightly owns the patent to an invention? This type of litigation often gets reported in the news and you need to understand both intellectual property [patents, trademarks, etc.] AND litigation.

Real Estate – You know the saying "Good fences make good neighbors?" Not always. Sometimes your neighbor thinks your property deed is wrong and you wind up in court. Understanding real estate help here.

Getting That First Job

You've finished your paralegal studies and you have a certificate and/or a bachelor's degree and you're ready to go to work. You polish up your resume and hop on Indeed and look for jobs. Unfortunately, every job ad says they want someone with experience already.

So how do you get experience?

There is no simple answer. You have to think outside the box. You have to decide immediately if you want to stay in the city where you live or expand your search area. That is a critical decision.

If you live in a large metro area like Atlanta, where I do, there are some advantages. There are many really large firms that will hire you to come in and be a receptionist, or an admin, or a billing clerk. Sometimes those positions are never even advertised because they get in so many resumes they can just pick and choose. You would do well to figure out the biggest law firms in your town and go online and figure out the emails or phone number for the Office Manager or head of HR and get in touch with that person. An old-fashioned phone call may work best. Emails are easy to ignore.

I worked at a very large, very prestigious law firm here in Atlanta and some of the paralegals there started off as Project Assistants. PA's would do things like bates stamp thousands of pages of records, or index depositions, or create binders full of records. (Sometimes larger firms call project assistants Interns.) If a huge batch of records needs to be sent to an expert witness, they may do that. It used to be a lot of paper shuffling and that has changed a lot over the years, but putting thousands of pages in a

Dropbox folder or on a thumb drive still takes time. That kind of work is a great way to get a foot in the door.

If you live in a medium-sized or small town, don't despair. Sole practitioners or attorneys in small firms are often willing to hire inexperienced people and train them. The unfortunate part is those tiny firms figure they can get away with paying newbies much less, or not offering benefits. You can take a job answering the phone or handling intake calls (from prospective clients) and then get promoted.

Law firms will often hire paralegals without the exact kind of experience they want IF the candidate has experience in a related field. For instance:

- Court clerks
- Medical office employees
- Mediation company coordinators
- Insurance company clerks or admins
- Government workers, for instance employees of the Department of Labor

Litigation paralegals who have experience as nurses or even CNAs will usually have no trouble finding paralegal work. A Nurse Paralegal often makes more money than a regular Litigation paralegal, especially for firms that do personal injury or medical malpractice cases. Nurse paralegals basically spend their time reviewing medical records and creating summaries or chronologies and often can work from home.

Social media can be very helpful in finding a job. Lawyers and paralegals have many Facebook pages and you can sometimes get leads on good jobs there. I got a recent job by finding a Facebook page for lawyers in my town and posting on there that I am a very experienced paralegal needing work, and I got a contract position. They liked me and after a few months I was hired full-time. I've seen others post who are not very experienced but they get jobs, too, mainly because it's easier and faster than a lawyer posting an ad. Lawyers network on social media all the time.

Call placement firms in your town. Robert Half is a well-known legal placement firm with many offices. I've gotten many contract jobs through them, and some permanent jobs. Many firms will only work with experienced paralegals but if you can get someone on the phone, ask for their advice. Sometimes law firms don't even use specialized placement firms, but they will call a general placement firm to hire an admin or a receptionist. Call ALL the placement firms in your town if you want to be thorough.

Never underestimate the power of networking. In my first job, the firm hired a "paralegal" who had never worked in a law office or been to paralegal school but her father was a golf buddy of one of the attorneys. I had to train her, starting off by explaining how a lawsuit worked. That sort of thing still happens, especially in smaller towns.

You may have to think really far outside the box. For instance, your parents' neighbor is an attorney. Print out a nice copy of your resume and walk next door with some homemade brownies, and chat. Offer to do an unpaid internship for a few weeks, to prove yourself. Even if there are no openings at your neighbor's firm, ask the attorney to email your resume to his or her attorney friends. You never know what might happen.

Worst case scenario, take any job you can get, but keep looking for paralegal work. Don't give up.

What Exactly IS Your Job?

Early in my career, there were attorneys – some of whom were at my firm – who had no idea what a paralegal was supposed to do, and therefore felt it was perfectly fair to ask me to do anything.

For example, at the first law firm where I worked, the attorneys never used courier services and I was asked to drive an hour north and file pleadings in the courthouse several times because they couldn't be mailed. The attorney (let's call him Mike) liked to wait until the actual day a brief was due and then start on it, and walk into my office at 2 or 3 p.m. and say "This has to be in LaFollette before 4:30, so as soon as my secretary gets it ready to go, you need to get in the car and take it up there."

The first time Mike asked me to do it, I quietly freaked out. I had never been to LaFollette. I had no idea where it was, or where in town to find the courthouse. There was no GPS then. I had to borrow a map and try to find LaFollette and figure out my route. When I got to town I had to stop and ask someone for directions to the courthouse. Then I had to park and feed a meter with change. Then I had to go inside and find the correct office and hope the clerk would accept the pleading. Sometimes courts had weird rules, like they would only accept long paper, or they needed two copies (one for the judge), etc. I made several trips to LaFollette over the course of maybe 6 months, and then came a dreadful day, the day when Mike really waited until the last minute and he walked in and said "OK, it won't be ready until an hour before the courthouse closes, but just speed going up there and if you get stopped, I'll pay the ticket."

Now, I was a bit of a leadfoot in my youth, and I knew that if I speeded and got caught, it would delay me 10-20 minutes and the clerk's office would likely be closed when I got there. I told Mike I would take it, but I was not willing to speed. He couldn't get the points off my license if I got caught. He was not happy to hear it, and I was a little afraid I would get fired, but I felt like he was being unreasonable. Long story short, he asked the runner, who was a college student, to do it. The runner took the filing up to LaFollette. I didn't get fired. I was rather relieved when Mike quit and went to another firm, though.

There may be times when an attorney asks you to do something that might endanger your car or yourself and you will have to make a difficult judgment call as to whether or not to do it, but fortunately, those instances tend to be rare, particularly nowadays when most pleadings are filed electronically.

When I started my first job, my father worked in the bank in the same building and he used to give me a lot of advice, most of it very sound. He always said never use the phrase "that's not my job." As he used to say, if they are paying you, it's your job. I've worked for attorneys who asked me to do the job of their secretary when she called in sick, and if I had said "that's not my job" that would have been considered at best an example of not being a team player, at worst insubordinate. I've done the job of the receptionist, the runner, the secretary, and the catering manager, as needed. I've been a travel planner, an event planner, and the holiday card writer. I've written the office newsletter. Most attorneys feel that everyone has to pitch in to achieve the common goal.

Just for fun, here is a partial list of things I've done that were not my job:

- typed up letters and pleadings from dictation
- acted as the receptionist when she called in sick
- picked up an attorney from the car dealership
- fetched lunch for an attorney

- washed dishes in the kitchen
- decorated the firm Christmas tree
- picked up an attorney's dry cleaning
- ordered and picked up lunch for everyone in a deposition
- picked up an attorney's child from daycare
- sewed a button on the shirt of an attorney just before a hearing
- watched a toddler while her mother was in deposition
- driven an attorney home after his car wouldn't start
- addressed holiday cards
- Delivered holiday gifts to clients
- picked up witnesses and drove them to the courthouse
- bought an attorney's wife her Christmas gift on Christmas Eve
- bought cold medicine for an attorney who was in trial
- went to an attorney's house and got her small TV (so she could show a video in court) and took it to the courthouse
- straightened up an attorney's messy desk right before a client meeting
- spent all day cleaning an attorney's office, putting filing back in folders and reassembling files, dusting, taking out the trash etc. to get ready for a client meeting

As in the speeding example already mentioned, the possible exceptions are if you're asked to do something illegal (like speeding) or immoral. If that happens, seriously consider finding another job. (In my years as a paralegal I was never asked to do anything even remotely immoral, just fyi.)

GENERAL TIPS

Be nice, no matter tired or stressed out you are. Part of being a professional is learning how to control your emotions. Examples: That secretary you just snapped at might be the person who can save your butt when something needs to be filed or snail mailed out at the last minute. That court clerk you were just snotty to on the phone might "accidentally" not see that order you need the judge to sign today. That law clerk you are snippy to might get hired and be your boss next year.

Don't act all high and mighty and superior. Ever.

Always have paper and pen handy when you pick up the phone. Whether you are making a call or taking a call, there's a 90% chance you will need to make notes. Example: the client calls to say they are back in the hospital and likely to be there a week or so. You need to write down the date, who called, why, the name of the file, the name of the hospital. Then you need to tell the attorney, or at least send an email. He will likely tell you to do a memo to the file. Then you need to note somewhere in the file that the plaintiff's most recent records will need to be requested, and calendar to follow up on that.

Never assume anything. Assumptions will get you in trouble every time. If you're unsure, ask. Example: Don't assume the attorney knows you're bad at math and will re-check your math on anything. He is just as likely to assume you are a math whiz and not check anything, and when your math is pointed out as being wrong in a deposition or in a hearing or [God forbid] a trial, guess who will get blamed? YOU.

Develop a strong stomach. Example: I went to work for an insurance defense attorney years ago and after about 4 years she started doing a lot of plaintiff's work in wrongful death cases. Her whole practice changed. I started having to look at lots of autopsy photos – grisly photos with blood and guts visible. Sometimes I had nightmares about those photos.

Sometimes I had nightmares about talking to her right after trial and being blasted in the face by her *trial breath*. Gift your attorney with a roll of mints right before trial, if you have to be near her during that stressful time.

Become a skilled diplomat. I once had to listen to an attorney complain about her husband for an hour, and although I agreed wholeheartedly, I had to maintain a poker face because I knew she would get over being mad at him but she would never forget it if I told her what a jerk he was. [This is actually good life advice: never badmouth one spouse to another.]

Be so organized that if you drop dead tomorrow, it will be easy to pick up where you left off. This means keeping your files, your notes, and everything you do meticulously organized and documented. Example: you are really sick and at home with a fever, and your attorney calls and says I'm writing a brief and I have to know, did you interview that witness? And you reply: "Yes, but I have not written up the formal memo memorializing that. Look in the file folder paralegal notes and memos and you will see my notes, scanned into a PDF and labeled Joe Smith interview 2.21.23."

TIP: When I was reviewing medical, school, or employment records for my last boss I would copy any PDF pages that contained something particularly useful and just pop all the pages in a folder labeled Hot Docs [a folder on the computer, not paper]. The attorney knew when he was prepping for a deposition or hearing he could find that folder on the computer and see exactly what I recommended he review. An example would be a medical record where the plaintiff – who sued our client saying he had a back injury -- complained of back pain a year before our accident.

Understand and accept that just like law schools don't prepare attorneys to practice, many paralegal programs don't really prepare you for your day-to-day work life. Example: I spent hours working on a brief in paralegal school. I've never once had an attorney ask me to write a brief. I've never been asked to do real legal research. The only related tasks I've ever been given were to cite check a brief or to find and read court rules. Now, I think paralegals today are much better trained and may be asked to do legal research, and hopefully will be able to do it competently. Just keep in mind that a formal paralegal education may or may not help you when it comes to something like organizing your day.

TIP: If you can plan your day and get your attorney trained to understand the importance of your keeping to that schedule, it will make life easier. I used to return calls and emails in the morning and save projects like medical chronologies and deposition indexes for the afternoon.

Never mention your opinions on religion or politics, no matter how informal your office may be. This can be tricky. Example #1: If the attorney sees you leaving in a car with a bumper sticker on it endorsing a particular candidate, the attorney may think you're an idiot for voting for that guy, and want to debate it with you, which is never a good idea. Example #2: You mention that your brother has a husband, and your supervising attorney, who is a very conservative Christian, decides he'd rather have another conservative be his paralegal, and he finds an excuse to terminate you or move you to a different team.

Don't use your cell phone while at work. Keep it put away and on silent. At one of my corporate jobs a paralegal asked in her interview how much time was allowed for her to be on her cell phone every day. She didn't get hired, needless to say.

Never mention you are looking for another job. It's just not a good idea, no matter how much you like your supervisor, or how informal the office may be. Example: you mention you need more money and you're looking, and your supervisor then makes you so miserable you quit -- and you will be unlikely to get unemployment.

TIP: Don't tell the office manager or your fellow paralegals or anyone else if you are looking for another job. Just keep it to yourself until you are ready to give notice.

Proofread! Bad grammar, wrong spellings, incorrect punction – all look unprofessional. The computer will not catch everything. Grammarly will not catch everything. AI will not catch it. Sometimes the attorney will misspell something repeatedly. Example: I read a pleading where the attorney repeatedly said "in the coarse and scope of her employment" -- and I had to explain to the attorney why the word "coarse" was the wrong one to use there. The secretary had not caught it. If you are not good at English, educate yourself. Paralegals must be able to write well.

Return your phone calls. Check emails and phone messages every single day, and return them within 24-48 hours, even if the email says "I can't make this a priority right now but I can assure you I will revisit it by the end of the week."

TIP: It's a good visual reminder to write an email to yourself regarding every phone message, but don't open the email until you're returned the call.

TIP: Never leave an outgoing voicemail greeting that says "I will return your call at my earliest convenience." It sounds really obnoxious.

Sit in on a deposition, at least once. Early in my career, I was told I would have to chauffeur my attorney to a deposition because his car had died. I had a lot of work to do and was kind of irritated but it turned out to be a great learning experience. Watching a skilled litigator coax information out of a witness was fascinating. I also took notes during the deposition and the attorney told me later they were useful. The very next day I was able to start the process of getting some additional medical records, and tracking down some witnesses we hadn't known about, without having to wait for a memo from the attorney or a review of the deposition transcript.

Don't work too fast. It's better to be slower and have fewer mistakes. As you learn, you will get faster. I've had to clean up messes made by other paralegals who valued speed over quality and I was not able to bill for it.

If you figure out a more efficient way to do something, tell the attorney. I worked for an attorney a few years ago whose files never had a chart listing where the requests for documents had been sent, or whether or not we ever got a response. There are computer programs who do that too, but he didn't utilize one of them either. I started making a chart for every file and made sure he knew where to find the chart so he could see what records we had gotten in and which ones were not in yet.

When it comes to file organization and tracking of materials or tasks, there are technologies that may help, too. Younger attorneys may be open to the idea of using a program like Sharepoint or Monday, but do your research on those types of companies on your own time.

Make communication a priority. Attorneys are super vigilant about time, and they usually don't want to have to stop and explain something to you but sometimes you have to diplomatically make them do just that. If an assignment is confusing, go back to the attorney with it and make him explain it better.

Things to keep in your purse or desk. Paralegals need to be prepared for anything.

- Motrin (or whatever you take for a headache)
- Tums (or whatever you take for indigestion).
- A small sewing kit, in case you pop a critical button. I once had to sew a button on a lawyer's shirt right before he had a hearing. (Also, showing cleavage or side boob or wearing see-through shirts is NOT a good idea in a law office, so fix your own popped button when necessary!)
- Bottled water, because hydration is important and you might have to drive across town to pick up your attorney at a car dealership.
- Period supplies. Females, always have pads and tampons for emergencies.
- Pretty making stuff: hairbrush, lipstick, etc. in case a client comes in unexpectedly or you have to take something to the attorney who is in the courtroom.

Networking is important. If there is a paralegal organization in your town, join it. There are Facebook groups for paralegals and you can find some useful tips and information in those groups. If you're looking for a job, networking can be really valuable.

Find out if you will be asked to do legal research. I've never worked for an attorney who asked me to do research. I've cite checked and checked local court rules, but that's about it. However, most paralegal programs today include better instruction on research, so find out from day one what your attorney expects.

Overtime can be tricky. If you need to work overtime, make sure the attorney knows you are doing it. Not all clients will pay for overtime and you can get in trouble if it's not pre-authorized.

If it's a firm with more than a couple of paralegals, get a mentor. A paralegal mentor is essential, even if you've been a paralegal for a few years. She [or he] can help you understand office procedures and politics and get your billables where they need to be.

Go above and beyond what you are asked to do. For instance, you are tasked with reviewing thousands of pages produced in discovery and noting which ones should be used as exhibits. Offer to do a chronology, which will best be done with a chart. Offer to do another chart of potential exhibits. Always be aware of opportunities to make yourself more useful.

Know Your Attorney[s]

Just like any other group of humans, attorneys are not all the same. Some attorneys are chatty and laid back, and some aren't. Some will treat you like a secretary. Some will treat you like a law clerk. Some will get ticked off if you show up 5 minutes late, but some won't. Some will think it's okay to call you at home at 10 at night. Some like to yell and scream.

If you are working for one or two attorneys -- working closely with them -- you are smart to get to know your attorneys as much as possible. Adapt to how they like things done. Make suggestions but don't be pushy and insistent.

Attorneys usually are under a lot of pressure. They typically leave law school with a boatload of student debt. They need to repay the debt, help grow the firm, and meet billable hourly goals. If they work at a small firm they often are asked to entertain clients, and/or pressured to participate in firm activities even if they have a mountain of work to do. If they have spouses and children they are trying to find a doable work/life balance and that can be very hard at the beginning of a law career. If it's a sole practitioner, he or she will have all the responsibility and worry of making sure all the bills get paid every month, including your salary.

After I had been working as a paralegal for about a year, my dad came to me and said he would pay the tuition if I wanted to go to law school. I thought about it for maybe 10 seconds and said no way. I had seen how hard the young lawyers worked and I didn't want that life. I admire attorneys who are successful at juggling work and home life, though. It takes skill.

Here are a few tips on how to get to know and get along with your supervising attorneys:

What's their work style? Do they like to work ahead, or wait until the last minute? Do they proofread and edit your work carefully or just assume you got it right? If you have a hard time figuring them out, ask another paralegal or an admin that has been there a while. They may tell you something important like "His wife just had their first baby so he isn't getting a lot of sleep." In that case, try to be extra helpful and forgiving.

I once volunteered to babysit for an attorney so he and his wife could have a "date night." He was very grateful. Unfortunately, they still got divorced about a year later, but I had tried to help.

Find out what your attorney did before law school. If he was a paralegal, he may be a great source of practical help. If he was a claims adjustor, he can explain insurance stuff to you. If he has an MBA he can explain business records in a corporate matter. Etc.

Find out when your attorney's birthday is and calendar it on your calendar. Bring in a card, or a cupcake, or in some way acknowledge it. Most people appreciate birthday cheer.

Ask if you can sit down and meet with your attorney periodically to go over your cases and see what needs to be done. This will help you learn their work style and keep up with your assignments, and it's generally a good idea. Sometimes you can bill for that type of meeting, so be sure and ask about that.

Never gossip about your attorney. It's not a good idea to gossip anyway, but particularly not about the attorneys. Example: You tell a fellow paralegal your attorney is getting a divorce. That paralegal you just told may go right to him and say what you said - because she hates her supervising attorney and wants to work for *your* supervising attorney, and she's happy to throw you under the bus to do it. Attorneys hate office gossip by the staff.

TIP: If you work for more than one attorney and cannot meet the deadlines because all of them are throwing work at you at once, go back to the attorneys and say "I'm sorry, but I need you to talk to the other attorneys and decide my priorities." They may grumble but it's a reasonable request. Learn how to stand up for yourself in a polite and firm way, without whining or getting too emotional.

Calendaring

Calendar like your life depends on it, because it does. Attorneys get very uptight about their calendars. I've never known one who was laid back about the calendar. If you get a call from your attorney telling you his child is sick and he cannot do a deposition tomorrow, be able to find that calendar entry in 10 seconds so you know what case, who to call, and what to do.

If your attorney misses a site inspection or a document production or a witness meeting because you forgot to calendar it, you will be lucky if you don't get fired.

If you keep charts regarding all depositions in a particular folder you can go straight to the chart and immediately call or email everyone [see next section on depositions].

When you first start to work for an attorney here are some good general questions to ask:

Do you put personal stuff on your calendar or not? If they say no, ask if you can note it somewhere else. I used to always keep a paper calendar for my own personal stuff and sometimes I would put my attorney's personal notes on there, too. Example: When I worked for a Jewish attorney I always marked the Jewish High holy days on my calendar so I would know she wouldn't be coming to work that day. Whatever the religion, mark down your attorney's vacation days and personal days somewhere. In Outlook there's a way to see your attorneys personal time off but it's not visible to the whole firm, which is great.

How far in advance do you like to prepare? Always think ahead. Make it a habit to look at the next day and the next week. You want to make sure you have time to do everything. Example: you need to find and label deposition exhibits for depositions on

Monday, so unless you want to work on the weekend, make sure that's done before Friday at 5 (or whenever you leave). Example: I got in trouble once because some records were scanned into the file and I didn't review and add them to a chronology before the plaintiff's deposition was taken. The attorney didn't get mad at the person who scanned them in and failed to tell me about them. He got mad at me. I should have been looking ahead on the calendar and double-checking the responses to all records requests at least a few days before the deposition.

Can you talk me through how you like to keep your calendar? Most attorneys will do this, because they want it done correctly.

How will I know if one of your cases gets on a trial calendar? Some attorneys let the admin handle that. Some attorneys are pretty casual if a case is #20 or higher. You need to discuss trial calendars, accessibility of local court rules, and how they like to handle that. Example: an attorney may want you to call all the attorneys on the cases ahead of theirs on the calendar and find out how likely they are to settle.

Learn the software. Newer or bigger firms usually have software that does your calendaring for you. Outlook is what's used at my current job and it's great, but there are a lot of programs out there. If you're a newbie, make it a priority to learn the calendaring software asap.

Deposition Preparations

A deposition is when a witness in a case answers questions under oath, and the questions and answers are recorded by a court reporter. Oftentimes now they are also captured on video. Depositions are very important. Cases can be won or lost based on deposition testimony.

Some attorneys split up the deposition chores between their admin and their paralegal. For instance, the admin may book the court reporter but the paralegal may prepare all the exhibits. Below, the assumption is the paralegal will do everything.

Younger attorneys may want to arrange their own depositions and may just ask you to do the notice. That's great. You just find another notice and use it as a "go by." Change the case style (if it's from a different case) and the details (who, when, where) and make sure the court reporter has been booked.

Older attorneys will often just tell or email you some dates and the name of the witness and leave everything else up to you. Deposition planning can take up a boatload of your valuable time if you don't have a good system in place. It's also important to know if you can bill for the time you spend coordinating everything.

These are important things to ask the attorney when he first tells you to start setting up depositions:

1. Names of deponents and whether they are being voluntarily deposed. [If not, you may need to prepare subpoenas.]
2. Roles in case [Example, wife of guy hurt in wreck, was in back seat / expert witness / manager of store where fall happened].
3. Is the deposition for discovery or evidence?

4. Will you do the notice or the administrative assistant?
5. If it's our witness, how do you want them prepped, call or in-person meeting? How long should I block off for that [an hour? Longer? How far in advance of the deposition?]
6. If the witness has to drive in for an hour, will the firm reimburse him for travel expenses?
7. Video needed? Will the court reporter arrange it or will we need to find a videographer?
8. How quickly do we need the transcript?
9. Do you already know what you want to use as exhibits?

Most attorneys who have been practicing a while have set up a particular way they like to do depositions. Learn it. I've had attorneys who wanted every exhibit in a particular folder 48 hours in advance. I've known attorneys who said they wouldn't start preparing until 4 p.m. the day before the deposition. My last attorney liked me to come up with suggested deposition questions and email them to him the day before.

Exhibits are very important. Always ask the attorney what they want to use as exhibits. If the case is about a car accident, for example, typical exhibits will be photos of the wrecked cars, the police report, medical records of those injured. If it's a business case exhibits might be different versions of a contract, or bank records.

Most attorneys like to use the same court reporter over and over, so find out who that is, and whether or not you're supposed to book them or the admin is supposed to do it. Also get a 2nd and 3rd choice so if the 1st choice is booked up you aren't in a panic.

If the deposition is going to be recorded by video, make sure that the court reporter is advised of that.

If the deposition requires a trip out of town, find out if you need to make travel arrangements or if the attorney will do that himself, or perhaps the admin.

At my last paralegal job I kept charts on each deposition, in a folder called Deposition Planning. Below is an example.

The 411:

ATTORNEYS	COURT REPORTER	PARTY DEPOSED	NOTES
[pltf] Joe Blow Dewey Cheatam and How 489 Main Street Anywhere, GA 30090 706-789-7890 jblow@ DCH.com paral. Jody Jones	Speedy Reporting 770-567-5678	Sandy Sanders	Sandy is hard of hearing; atty needs to not shout, though Sandy's son has to drive her and his name and cell number are:
[co-def] Howie Howard Big Bus Ads Law Firm 456 Peachtree St. Atlanta, GA 12345 hhoward@ BBA.com 404-567-5678			Howie likes to prepare the weekend before, so make sure everything is done by COB Friday

Paral: Amy Damey Admin: Sherry Day			

Depo. Dates and Availability

PARTY	ATTORNEY AVAILABILITY	PROPOSED DATE AND TIME	LOCATION	NOTES
Sandy Sanders [all day]	JB: April 3, 5, 10 HH: April 10, 11, 12, May 10	April 10	Radisson Hotel conf. room	Howard has a trial April 10-13 but it will likely settle
Tiny Thomason [half day]	JB: April 5, 6, 21, May 21 HH: May 21, 22	May 21	Pltf.'s firm	Make sure to attach photos as exhibits!

It's good to keep all depositions in a folder [Deposition Transcripts] and also to have this chart immediately visible as soon as you open the folder.

When you get in deposition transcripts, if there are more than a few, it may be a good idea to make a chart or spreadsheet. You may have to change the orientation to landscape. It should have the following columns:

Deponent's name

Date Taken

List of Exhibits

Indexed?

Court Reporter Contact Info?

Errata Sheet to Court Reporter?

I tend to do things old school but many firms have software to store and categorize depositions. Be sure to learn everything you need to know about deposition storage for that particular software.

TIP: If the deponent is the plaintiff in a personal injury case, get all the medical records in and the chronology done before the deposition. Remind your attorney to review the chronology as to which records they want to use for exhibits.

TIP: If you're trying to arrange for depositions in a small town where none of the attorneys have offices, here are some places where you might can rent a room: the court reporting firm's offices, hotels, libraries, restaurants (better to book between meals).

Indexing or Summarizing Depositions

There are many different ways to summarize a deposition. I have done summaries that read like essays. I've done summaries that were really indexes, listing the page and line and then the note. I've done subject matter summaries, although those are not needed much nowadays as most court reporters send word indexes that work as well or better. Every attorney has their own way they want to see a deposition summary done.

The first time an attorney says "Hey, summarize the depositions we just got in in the Smith case," your immediate reply should be "How do you like those done? Is there an example in another file I can look at and use as a go-by?"

The whole point is that instead of the attorney flipping through the first ten pages he can instead see something like this:

PAGES	LINE	NOTE
2-7		Joe Smith was born 8/7/1967 in Little Rock Arkansas and has lived in Hot Springs since he was 5 years old. Currently he lives at 1234 Jones Road in Smithville.
2	3-8	Joe never saw the pickup truck that struck his Honda Odyssey but felt the impact on the passenger's side and lost control when his wife screamed and was pushed into him.
5	1-25	Joe graduated from high school and attended DeVon's HVAC School and has worked in HVAC repair ever since.

TIP: Your attorney has a deposition of a witness, Carl Bond, next week. You pull out the other witness depositions and find where Carl Bond is mentioned. You draft a memo with a chart showing all mentions of Carl Bond in all the other depositions. This saves the attorney a lot of time – but get approval before you do it the first time. If the attorney is planning to do it himself because that's how he always preps, there's no need to duplicate work.

Example:

WITNESS	PAGE IN DEPO	NOTE
Jane Dye	78	Jane saw Carl spill water on the floor an hour before Plaintiff fell.

Medical Records

Some firms will have an entire team that does nothing but medical records, so if that's your situation, awesome. I've never worked at a firm where that was the situation. However, at most firms there's a system in place for medical records and you need to learn it.

The first thing to know is who does what. At most jobs, I've done it all – made the list, sent out the requests, calendared to follow up, put the records in the file, and created a chronology. That's not the only way to do it, though. Example: your job is to make a list of doctors and hospitals where plaintiff has treated and get it to the admin and she will send out the requests or subpoenas.

Phases of medical records gathering:

1. **Identify who to send requests to.** Example: Plaintiff has hurt her back in a car accident. Attorney John wants requests sent to every place the plaintiff has ever treated for anything, ever, so John wants her OBGYN records from twenty years ago. However, attorney Marianne only wants pertinent records since the accident, so only treatment for her back.

2. **List the records** somewhere. I like charts, but others may prefer spreadsheets. Then when the records come in, I note it on the chart or spreadsheet. So when the attorney says "How are we doing on getting the records?" you can whip out your chart and give him exact information.

   If your firm uses spreadsheets or a particular type of software to track this, learn it asap.

Date Request Sent	Name of Medical Provider	Address of Medical Provider	Records received?	Bates'd and Scanned in?	Added to Chronology?

TIP: It's a good idea to call medical providers and find out how they handle records requests before you send the request or subpoena. If you can address it to the attention of the person who actually handles the records you will likely get the records faster. If you can fax the request to that person it usually really speeds up the process. If a hospital uses a service like Ciox to copy records (most do, nowadays) you can figure that your request won't be processed quickly, and even if there are only 2 pages of records the cost will be at least $25-40.

As you get in records, give them a quick review and see if they mention other providers. For example, if it's mentioned that plaintiff hurt her back 5 years ago and treated with Dr. Smith at So-and-so clinic, get those records.

Make sure you know if you need to bates stamp records as they come in. Not all attorneys bates stamp. Smaller cases with just a few providers may not need records bates'd. If records are to be bates stamped find out how the attorney likes it done. Make sure you know how to bates a PDF.

3. Make a **Summary or Chronology** of treatment. There are many different ways to do those. Find out if the firm has a particular way all those chronologies are done. A lot of attorneys are very particular about how they like medical summaries or chronologies done, so talk to them about that. Some firms use charts, some use spreadsheets. Some use AI. I prefer to just make charts in Word.

4. **Keep reviewing records** and depositions as they come in, for names of other medical providers where you might need to get records.

5. Keep a **list of the charges** incurred with each doctor visit and therapy visit and hospitalization. Keep it updated. Make sure you're looking at records from after the accident.

TIP: Check the name and date of treatment every time you get in records. I once reviewed a set of pharmacy records that were already in the file, just after I was hired. They were for the wrong person with a similar name! The dates of birth didn't match. Neither the associate or the admin caught it, and records requests were sent out to several doctors who responded they'd never had the plaintiff as a patient. A lot of time was wasted (before I was hired) all because nobody realized the records were those of the wrong person.

TIP: Make notes for each medical provider such as "ask for Wanda, she handles the requests" or "They use Chartswap" or "doctor charges $25 plus $1.00 per page for responses." Some medical offices are not open on Friday, or they close for lunch for two hours a day and turn off the phones. What if you wait until Friday afternoon to call and ask them to fax you the latest office visit record, but they are closed and the deposition is Monday morning?!

Interrogatories and Requests for Production of Documents

Two of the most important ways to build a case are through Interrogatories and Requests for Production of Documents. Most of your really important information about treatment, witnesses, expenses, lost earnings, etc. will be in your ROG [Interrogatory] and RPD [Requests for Production of Documents] responses.

Although 90% of attorneys will ask you to respond to and/or draft discovery, that's not always the situation. My last attorney supervisor said only his associate would ever draft discovery or respond to it.

If you work at a firm where they use one of the newer AI programs to respond to discovery [for example, LegalMation] then your job is a lot easier. However, you will need to read through and edit discovery responses because AI doesn't always get all the details right, so there will still be work for you to do there.

Many firms don't use those types of programs yet, however.

Questions to ask when you're told to respond to discovery:

When are these due?

Can I call the client about what we need from them? [some attorneys don't want a paralegal calling a client]

Do you generally try to turn over whatever they ask for, or do you not like to turn over anything? [if you've been working with an attorney for a while you can obviously skip this one]

Re-copy each interrogatory or request, or just type out the responses?

Is there a list of standard objections you like to use?

If the attorney likes to respond "These records will be produced at a mutually convenient time and place" find out how the attorney wants that done.

If you are going to object on the basis of privilege, go ahead and start a privilege log?

Is there a file similar to this one where I can find a good go-by to use?

Drafting discovery to send to the other side, questions to ask the attorney:

Are there standard boilerplate pleadings I can start with?

Is there anything unique to this case you want to request?

If opposing counsel needs more time to respond do you generally grant it?

Some firms use a particular computer program or even an outside service to draft discovery, but your help may still be needed. For instance, you may need to keep track of whether or not the discovery gets done on time.

TIP: Make sure and calendar when you need to get discovery responses done or when the opposing party needs to have responses back to you. Pay attention to things like the attorney taking off sick or vacation days, and whether or not they are willing to review drafts on the computer when they are out of the office. In today's world most firms are going paperless, which is great, but the paralegal still needs to be very organized.

NOTE: When you get in discovery responses from opposing counsel you can be really helpful and save your attorney a lot of time by reviewing them and doing a memo with all the pertinent information culled from the responses. That way, instead of having to page through tons of objections and boilerplate the attorney can see, at a glance, exactly what new information was included. You should also offer to send out more documents requests if the responses tell you about some providers you didn't know about before.

Acronyms:

ROGS = Interrogatories

RPDs or RFPs = Requests for Production of Documents

RFAs = Requests for Admission [these are often sent at the same time as ROGS and RFPs]

Billing

If you are a defense paralegal you will need to master the art of billing and make it a priority from day one. Most firms have paper or computerized billing guidelines, and you need to familiarize yourself asap.

If you forgot to ask about the billable hourly requirement before you were hired, ask asap on your first day.

Make sure you know how soon after training you will be expected to start meeting the billable hourly requirement.

Always figure out quickly how much unbillable work you will be asked to do, and how many hours a day you will need to put in to meet your requirement.

On your first day in the office, ask if you can help other teams get ready for trial, because that weekend work can help you meet your goal. Example: I worked for an attorney years ago who never wanted me to help another team, and I quickly realized I had too much unbillable work to be able to meet my goal, so I had to reluctantly polish up my resume and start jobhunting again.

It's always a good idea to show your attorney some of your billing entries right after you start, to see if they want you to use different wording. Oftentimes they will say "no, the client won't accept that, here's how you need to word it." It's a lot easier to correct time entries daily rather than to try and go back a week or a month later, after you've forgotten even doing the task.

TIP: Keep a pad of paper and manually write down each case you work on, and the time, and later you can fix proper time entries before you leave for the day. You may work on the Smith case from 10-10:27 and then get a call and have to turn your attention to another case from 10:27-10:55. Then you may work on Smith again from 12:56-1:22. At the end of the day you look back through your notes and realize you've spent a total of 116 minutes on Smith. A lot of bigger firms use software for billing that allows you to set a timer on yourself, and those are really useful. If you get interrupted just his PAUSE, then resume again when you can.

TIP: A lot of clients won't pay for "block billing" so put down the exact time spent on each task. For example:

.4 reviewed deposition for treating doctors new to us

.5 drafted 2 new RPDs to medical providers General Hospital and Dr. Drake Remoray

.2 prepared correspondence to opposing counsel enclosing their copies of the RPDs

If you are working for a plaintiff's attorney it's a great idea to keep track of any work you do on a specific file, because sometimes, months down the road, your attorney may get awarded legal fees so he will have to have time records for himself and yourself, to submit to the court. An example would be writing demand letters, sending out records requests, etc. Oftentimes software like Clio makes it very easy to add time after a task is completed. Just ask the attorney if they want you to record time and do it after each task is completed.

Composing a billing entry can be tricky. Many clients like particular language. In general, you want to say:

What you did

Why you did it

Present tense

Example of a bad time entry:

Looked over medical records we got in from Dr. Smith.

Example of a good time entry:

Review and analyze patient file from Dr. Smith, to determine if information needs to be added to the medical chronology and if other providers are mentioned.

TIP: Ask to see typical billing entries for paralegals at the firm, to see how the proper wording.

Organizing Information

A big part of being a good litigation paralegal is figuring out ways to keep files well-organized. If you get hired by a big firm, they will likely have protocols in place for file organization and you will just learn them. At smaller firms, however, you might need to be proactive and get the files organized.

I learned years ago that the easiest way for me to be efficient and organized was to make charts. Spreadsheets are a pain in the butt, I think. Some paralegals and attorneys prefer them, however. I make charts of all medical records in chronological order, charts of employment records, charts of school records, etc. Chart Ideas:

- Charts showing every complaint of the plaintiff, with bates numbers of pages where he complained of pain even before our accident.

- Charts of all the names and addresses of the

NAME & ADDRESS	DEPO TAKEN?	OTHER DOCUMENT?	DAMAGING STATEMENTS	AVAILABILITY FOR TRIAL?
Jack Smith 1234 Hope Road Decatur, Georgia 30030 770-899-7892	Yes, 4/22/22	Statement taken by police the day of accident; affidavit attached to motion for summary judgment	"I saw the pltf strike his head on the windshield"	Out of town entire month of July

witnesses - for example:

- A chart started early in the case showing possible trial exhibits.

Other information that might benefit from a chart, and suggested columns:

- possible **trial exhibits** [what, significance, where in file, bates numbers]
- **imaging** in file [pre-accident, post-accident, date, type of image]
- **videos** [who, what, where, why, when, do we have a copy?]
- **graphics for trial** [type, what it shows, source]
- **travel arrangements** [date, reason for travel, flight info, hotel info, court reporter]
- **motions** [why it was filed, when it was filed, if it was granted]

Expert Witnesses

It's becoming more and more common to use expert witnesses in litigation, and it's super important to track what has been sent to them. Some experts will let you put everything in Dropbox or a similar site. Some experts are okay with getting a thumb drive. Believe it or not, some experts still want paper copies of everything.

For experts who want paper, it's a good idea to find a copying business in town who specializes not only in making copies but will also put them in tabbed notebooks for you. You might have to have a long phone conversation or send detailed instructions in an email but it will save a lot of your time in the long run.

Expert witnesses deserve their own chart, if there is more than one, for example:

EXPERT NAME, ADDRESS	AREA OF EXPERTISE	Materials Sent?	SYNOPSIS OF OPINION
Dr. Mo Greene 22145 Godfather Ln Brooklyn, NY 10089 555-098-3459 Assistant, Kay	Construction sites signage	Yes, see chart in his folder	Inadequate signage caused the accident

For each expert, if there is a lot of stuff going to him, consider a chart like this:

DATE SENT	BATES NUMBER	TYPE OF MATERIAL	NOTES
4/25/21	Ghb789-799	Photos of wreck	Need to get copies of later photos
5/2/21	Wtstmt456-	Statements of witnesses	Send

	458	who saw the wreck	depositions when transcripts come in
5/5/21	HenHosp456-1098	Medical records for Henning Hospital	If updated records received, send them to expert

Some firms have a protocol that all expert witness information needs to be on a spreadsheet. No matter how the information is kept, just be sure and keep it up to date.

Finding People

When I first became a paralegal there were enormous books in our law library called City Directories, and we could look up people by name or by address. I could sometimes locate witnesses by using that. We had city directories going back many years. They were information treasure troves.

Skip ahead to today, and most millennials have never even used a physical phone book to look up someone's phone number. Landlines are, for most people, a thing of the past, so finding a cell number in a phone directory wouldn't happen anyway.

However, we do have great resources in social media, cameras, and even websites that specialize in finding people.

In a recent paralegal position, I realized that the attorney was paying a boatload of money to someone to locate a witness, and I could do a better job. I am not a social media whiz kid but I am not an idiot, and so I will share a few tips with you.

Facebook and Instagram

Don't laugh. I know most people under thirty are not using Facebook a lot, if at all, but if you don't have a personal account, get one. Use a pseudonym and you won't have to accept a friend request from your mama or your grandmother. It's easier to search Facebook if you have your own account.

A lot of people don't know Facebook has two privacy settings, one for the public and one for Friends only.

If you are trying to find someone with a common name like Bill Smith, just forget it. Hire a private investigator. However, if you are trying to find someone named Atlas Carpenter, put that in the Facebook search box. Maybe he won't have a Facebook account but that's okay. Sometimes people who don't have a Facebook account get tagged in the photo of someone who does have an account, like Cindy Warneke (remember that name). Let's say that happens and you see Atlas with a group of people and they are all at a club called Joe's in the City. Find the Facebook page or Instagram page for Joe's in the City and scroll through the photos and see if you see Atlas in other photos. Maybe he's a regular. Maybe not. Maybe since his friend Cindy Warneke tagged Atlas on Facebook you should look on her page and see if Atlas is tagged in other posts. Maybe not, but somebody named Joan Carpenter is tagged, so look on Joan's page – bingo. She is Atlas' sister and he's in other photos on her page. Maybe Joan says something about Atlas getting off work at Jiffy Lube in Lawrenceville to come to her birthday party. You call the two Jiffy Lubes in Lawrenceville and just casually say "Yo, Atlas working today?!"

Also look on LinkedIn. Maybe you find Atlas on LinkedIn and even though there's not much on there you at least see his employer, and you find him that way.

If you are a Defense paralegal and you want to check out the plaintiff's social media accounts, expect that their attorney has had them either shut down those accounts or change the privacy settings. Sometimes not, though. I did a Google search with the name of a plaintiff once and found where she posted her wedding video on YouTube. She was supposed to be completely disabled and homebound but there was video of her dancing at her wedding and looking just fine. That's when it was time to get that video copied and ready to use either in her deposition or in court.

Cameras

We also forget sometimes that most stores and many homes now have cameras. Let's say you get the video of a slip and fall in a grocery store and there is an eyewitness standing right nearby, clearly visible. Maybe his testimony will be valuable because he saw the fall from an angle the camera doesn't have. How do you find him? Perhaps he is a regular there. Perhaps the cashiers know him, maybe even remember his name. Find out who was working the cash registers at the time of the fall and talk to them. Maybe he's not a regular. Maybe he is an employee and he just got off a long shift and he didn't stick around to offer himself as a witness, but you show the manager the footage and the manager gives you his contact information.

It's important that when you first get in a new lawsuit where there is even a remote possibility of camera footage being available, you figure that out. A lot of businesses delete footage after a few weeks or a few months.

Also, if police are called they often have body camera footage, and you will need to subpoena that and get it in the file asap.

Many people have Instagram accounts. I once found the Instagram account of a plaintiff and it was public. He had posted a video he had shot while [he said on camera] he was going 80 mph on the Atlanta interstate. He was on the same interstate a few weeks later when he had the accident that was the subject of our lawsuit. It made for an interesting line of questioning in his deposition.

Getting Along

Note: I've always worked for very traditional, conservative firms. Smaller firms staffed with younger attorneys may overlook a lot of this behavior.

WHAT YOU **WANT** TO SAY	WHAT YOU **SHOULD** SAY INSTEAD	LESSONS LEARNED
I got so wasted last night!	Does anyone have any Motrin?	Keep Motrin in your purse or desk.
Are you really going to give me grief about being 5 minutes late?!	I'll try to leave home earlier so I will be on time.	Lost time means lost money for the firm. Always remember that.
There's no way I can meet this billable requirement!	Hey supervising attorney, can I set up a time to talk to you about how I can bring up my billable hours?	Never be casual about billing. Perhaps you should look for a job where billing time is not a requirement.
Do I have to go to the firm holiday party?	Nothing negative or whiny about the party.	They don't have to do anything for the holidays, so be glad they make an effort.
Hey, I heard Smith and Jones is hiring!	Nothing. Never say this out loud where an attorney [or anyone else] can hear you.	You never want to give the impression you're unhappy where you work, because you are going to lose the respect of the

		attorneys.
Hey there Office Manager, let me tell you the awful thing my attorney did!	Nothing. Never tell the office manager anything negative about an attorney, unless you want it to get back to the attorney.	The attorneys pay the office manager, not you.
That plaintiff is such a con artist!	If you work for a plaintiff's firm, say nothing. Otherwise, if you just have to comment be diplomatic: I see no justification for the level of disability the plaintiff is claiming.	The optimal paralegal demeanor is cool and detached. / It's always risky to malign one of the parties in front of the attorney, no matter which side you're on.
That's the ugliest tie I've ever seen!	What an interesting tie! Was it a gift?	I once teased an attorney about his tie, only to find out he was colorblind. Always err on the side of being kind.
Hey, since you're on vacation next week, can I park in your spot?!	Have fun on vacation and don't worry about anything! I will hold down the fort.	Attorneys feel nervous about going on vacation, so don't give them the impression you view it as a Get Out of Jail Free card.
How much is my Christmas bonus this year?!	Nothing. Those bonuses are entirely	Never go out and buy a bunch of gifts, assuming you

	discretionary.	will get a big bonus.
I'm going to get a neck/face tattoo!	Never say this.	Older folks and conservative folks really don't want to see neck or face tats. Even if you work for young lawyers, older clients may be put off by your appearance.

A Dozen Ways Paralegals Can Help Market Their Firms

Most attorneys are too busy practicing law to really brainstorm about marketing strategies and then implement them. If you think about it, anything that gets the name of your firm and your attorneys in the public eye can lead to new cases. Most people find the thought of hiring a lawyer to be very scary and intimidating, and they are wary of getting fleeced by an unscrupulous firm. Attorneys who are visible in their community are more likely to get hired.

Now, if you work for a large firm with offices in several cities, the attorneys may or may not be willing to listen to your ideas about marketing the firm. Large firms usually pay marketing directors to handle everything.

Paralegals and legal assistants at medium or small firms should think about finding ways to help the firm gain new clients, because the better the firm does, the better your career goes. If you need to go in and ask for a raise, it helps to be able to say something like "Remember that case we settled for $100,000 a few months ago? That plaintiff is my neighbor. Great guy!"

If you decide to help with marketing, make sure and speak to your attorney first. You may be able to put it on your timesheet as "firm related" or "new business" and not get penalized - or not. If they don't want it done during the regular workday, consider doing it on your own time.

As a general rule, if an attorney knows you are interested in helping do more than just your own particular job, it makes you look good, like a team player.

Here are a dozen ways you can assist with marketing your firm:

Sit down and talk to your supervising attorney about marketing. Oftentimes, attorneys don't give much thought to marketing the firm. The more interested you appear to be, and the more willing to go above and beyond your regular duties, to help out the firm, the better for your career.

Tell people where you work and what your firm does. Places where you can network:
Church functions
Facebook
Family Reunions
Neighborhood parties
PTSA Meetings
The gym

Offer to write blogs for the firm website. Usually, blogs are most effective when they link to other websites, and then summarize or expand on a news article. The more links, the better the search engines like the firm website. Or perhaps there's a new law that pertains to what you do. Offer to write up a summary of what the law says and post it as a blog or on social media.

Offer to help the attorneys find speaking engagements. One of the best ways for a firm to find clients is for the attorneys to be personable and approachable. Perhaps your church brings in speakers for seminars. Suggest that the church members might get a lot out of a speech from an attorney. Examples:
- The Importance of Making a Will
- 10 Things You May Not Know About Hiring An Attorney
- Have an idea for an invention? Let's talk about patenting it

Read websites or publications that address how attorneys can market themselves. If you see an interesting article that looks like it would be helpful, send your boss an email, or make a copy of the article and put it on his/her desk.

Help your attorneys network. A lot of small firms get cases from other attorneys, typically old law school classmates who practice in the same town. If you've worked at other firms and left on good terms, consider suggesting your old boss and your new boss go to lunch and discuss referral opportunities. Perhaps you have attorneys who are your neighbors, or an attorney is your Sunday School teacher. Introduce your attorney friends to each other.

Help with firm Client Appreciation events. For instance, the firm can send out tickets to a Braves or Falcons game to clients, then have a tailgate party ahead of time and transport everyone to the game in a bus. You can offer to prepare invitations, arrange for catering, design a firm tee shirt, etc.

Brainstorm ideas for items to post on the firm's Facebook or Twitter page. If the firm doesn't have social media accounts, offer to set them up. Once the Facebook or Twitter page is up and running, post links to it on your Facebook or Twitter account.

Firm tee shirts are a great way to advertise the firm in a subtle way. For instance, you are at the car wash wearing a tee shirt that says Smith Law Firm and has the firm catchprase on it "The lawyers who care." Someone standing behind you in line needs an attorney and observes you and you seem like a nice person. They ask you about what you do, and what kinds of cases the firm handles, etc. The next day they call and make an appointment to come in and discuss a case.

Research ways the firm can be more visible in the community. For instance, encourage folks in the firm to do a Habitat for Humanity build, or going on a Fun Run for charity, while wearing firm tee shirts.

Suggest your attorneys become more visible at schools in the area. Schools are always looking for financial help, and attorneys and businesses who help get known to the parents, who might need legal help and would be more likely to call the attorney they met at the school grounds Clean Up Day than a stranger.

These are some examples of ways to do that:
- Underwrite the cost of the baseball uniforms
- Put an ad in the program of the school play
- Sponsor an award for teachers, for example $100/month to the Teacher of the Month, or $500 at the end of the school year to the Teacher of the Year
- Fund a scholarship for a high school senior who is interested in going to law school

Suggest ways the firm can re-vamp their website. Most firms put up a website and there it sits, untouched, for years. Then the attorneys wonder why they never get calls from potential clients looking for legal representation on the internet. There are a number of companies that cater to law firms and will design websites for attorneys. If there is only a small budget, though, an independent website designer will be more economical. You can research possible website companies for your attorney.

Afterword

I kind of fell backwards into the profession because when I finished college I just couldn't find a job. Even though it was the 1980's jobs – particularly first jobs for new college graduates – weren't always easy to get. I had classmates in paralegal school with degrees in Computer Science, Business, etc. The program that was supposed to train us really wasn't great at dispensing practical advice. My main teacher was great because she often said "this is what you need to do when the attorney says update the corporate minute book." Etc. I was ready to hit the ground running as a corporate paralegal. Too bad I never got a chance to do that.

I have perused the course offerings for paralegal training programs today and I think most are far superior to the training I got, and that's awesome. Now, you can become a certified paralegal. You can take advanced courses. However, I question whether or not there are enough really practical guides like Paralegal 411. Most paralegal courses are taught by attorneys, who have never worked as a paralegal.

My course as a paralegal has never run smooth since 2009, when I was laid off from a corporate job. That's the trouble with those in house positions; you are more likely to get laid off in the event of an economic downturn.

I moved my mother in with me in 2005 and she helped me a lot with raising my kids, but then she herself became increasingly frail as time went on, and I couldn't hold down a regular paralegal office job and take care of her. I have an MA in Creative Writing so I started taking on writing jobs, which could be handled from home. Finally, in 2019, I got a work from home paralegal job, and it came in handy when Covid hit. Quarantining from home really didn't have much effect on my life. When my mom passed away, though, and I was ready to go back to work full-time I found the paralegal profession had changed a LOT.

The basics don't change, though. A paralegal still has to be super organized and efficient. She has to constantly embrace change and learn new techniques, skills, and computer programs. People skills will always be important. The first time I had to call and interview a witness I was a nervous wreck. It just takes practice to sharpen up those skills.

Attorneys nowadays are far more aware of the importance of work/life balance. They are far less likely to say anything racist/sexist/hurtful. That's awesome. I could have filed many EEOC complaints over the years but I never felt like it would be worthwhile or productive in the long run. Pick your battles wisely.

I hope you have gotten something out of this book. If so, feel free to recommend it to friends. If you've been working a while and have some good suggestions and you'd like to see them in future editions, email me at dethompson62@yahoo.com.

I've written a memoir called Talking Back, Stories from the Big Hair and Pantyhose Years, and it's available on Amazon. It includes a lot of stories about my first 15 years as a paralegal.

If you like to read fiction, check out my Amazon page because I have written a number of books and you will also find a list on the next page.

Dee Thompson
2024

My Education and Writing:

I earned a BA in Drama and an MA in Creative Writing and I have worked as a freelance writer, a journalist, and a paralegal. My essays have been included in the award-winning books Call Me Okaasan [2009] and The Divinity of Dogs [2013]. My seven novels are on Amazon, to wit: Ghosts in the Garden City [2019], Leaf Season [2019], Heart of My Own Heart [2020], Return to Marietta [2022], Dancing in the Wreckage [2023] The Wedding Conspiracy [2023], The Garland Belles [2024]. Additionally, I've published a cookbook, What's for Dinner, Mom? and I compiled and edited a posthumous memoir of my mother's writings, Singing to the Cows [2021]. I've published numerous articles online and in print, [portfolio] and I've been writing a personal blog, The Crab Chronicles, since 2005.

In December 2023 I published a memoir called Talking Back, Stories from the Big Hair and Pantyhose Years, and it's available on Amazon. It includes a lot of stories about my life, including childhood, dating, and my first 15 years as a paralegal.

www.ingramcontent.com/pod-product-compliance
Lightning Source LLC
Chambersburg PA
CBHW071047220526
45467CB00004B/1708